Vietnam
Socialist Republic
Stephen Platt

www.leveretpublishing.com

Vietnam: Socialist Republic
First published - April 2018
Published by
Leveret Publishing
56 Covent Garden, Cambridge, CB1 2HR, UK

Nón lá, Vietnamese traditional leaf hat

ISBN 978-1-9124602-0-5

© Stephen Platt 2018

All rights reserved. No part of this publication may be reproduced, stored in a retrieval system or transmitted in any form by any means, electronic, mechanical, photocopying, recording or otherwise, except brief extracts for the purpose of review, without the written permission of the publisher.

Vietnam
Socialist Republic

Vietnam 2018

Hanoi

Friday 9 March
It was all very sudden. Keiko emailed me four days ago to ask if I might be prepared to go to Vietnam to do a job for the World Bank. There is a mission to assess the damage and estimate reconstruction costs after a typhoon that hit the southern part of Vietnam last November and they were short of a housing specialist to do the estimates and make recommendations for building back better. I suggested she ring me. On the phone she explained that she was due to go herself but that there had been a typhoon in Tonga three weeks ago and she had pulled in the only person who could have been sent to Vietnam to help her. She also said it was highly unusual to do this kind of rapid assessment so long after the event.

She said she knew it was a long shot at such short notice, expecting me to say no. I said I would consider going and asked what was involved. She explained the process and said I'd have to write a proposal and get it back to her that day if there was any chance of my going. She sent me pro forma for the technical proposal, financial statement and organisational description. I asked how many days and told her my usual day rate. The issue was that this had to be a firm contract since to employ me as an individual would mean my resigning from CAR. She assumed we were already registered as World Bank suppliers because I'd told that we had submitted a proposal to assess Armenian schools a couple of years ago. If you're not already registered there is no chance, she said.

So I beavered away all day cloning the Armenian schools proposal and updating the details. And we negotiated the finance. I used to be Keiko's boss and she's Japanese so it must have been a little difficult for her, nevertheless we quickly settled on 20 days work. The World Bank would cover business class flights, which was an encouragement since I remembered how cramped I had been flying to Thailand in 2006 after the tsunami and only six months after my hip operation.

I needed a ballpark figure for the financial proposal. It would be expensive so soon before the flight, she said. I was keen to fly direct, but this seemed to be costing much more since only Vietnamese airlines flew direct from Heathrow to Hanoi. We settled on a ballpark figure of $5,000 for flights and I steamed ahead and got the proposal back to her in a couple of hours. Easy working with me, I texted. Yes, she replied. Then she sent me a load of files of previous reports and spreadsheets and I got a feel of what was required. Piece of cake, I texted; thought so, she said.

Saturday 10 March
I went downtown and bought a couple of pairs of trousers in a sale and short-sleeved shirts in M&S and I popped into Trailfinders and they found the only direct flights leaving on Tuesday the 13th and getting back on the 22nd in time to help Scharlie get the house ready for visitors that weekend. The problem was Trailfinders could only hold the tickets till 8 pm that day. Unfortunately I still didn't know if it was on and had to let the flights go as Keiko wasn't that encouraging that we could manage it, what with the different time zones and the weekend.

And then on Sunday she emailed to say we weren't registered and that there was no chance. As well as the procurement office in India having to approve the proposal, we now needed people in Washington to approve CAR's registration as a supplier. Keiko said we would need two years accounts

Huge hotel development all along beach north of Cam Ranh airport

and banks checks etc. I asked her to explain the procedure and she pointed me to the online registration. I said I'd have a go tomorrow.

Monday 12 March

I rang Anna, our company secretary at the time of the Armenia proposal, to see the issue remembered registering us. She couldn't help. I had a job remembering my personal ID and password to just get on to the World Bank website, but I managed it and managed to fill in all the registration forms. On Monday I spent the day getting ready to go and booked and paid for my flights even though it was a big risk. I'd asked Keiko who'd pay if it didn't go ahead and she said you! An expensive unplanned holiday, I thought. The business class seats had gone. There were only two left on Saturday when I'd provisionally booked with Trailfinders. I thought to change to another carrier with a stopover, but on an impulse asked if there was a premium economy seat left. In the event there was on the outward flight and business class on the return. It saved me money and I was all set. Just needed a miracle with the World Bank approvals process.

I spent the day printing out the material Keiko had sent me, together with

Luxury hotels built on the sand dunes

my boarding pass maps etc. I also went to Waterstones and bought a guide and a map of Hanoi and a book to read on the plane – Mary Beard's Rome. I also talked to Robin about a World Bank bid for Sri Lanka. Suddenly, after a dearth of work, there seems to be a glut.

I emailed people in the Risk Centre to say I couldn't make the meeting tomorrow and managed to get feedback from Oliver on the disaster recovery survey I'm planning to launch and made the edits and sent it off. I just need to deploy it properly which means identifying good contacts in each of the 13 to 14 countries we are case studying. Andy sent a nice email saying he was pleased I was going and that it would be useful for the study and I should give a talk when I got back.

My suite in the Intercontinental Hotel in Nha Trang

Nha Trang

Tuesday 13 March

And now I am on the plane, a couple of hours into the journey. I slept well, woke early and got to Heathrow uneventfully. I had a long chat with Farnaz over coffee and croissant. She's in Iran visiting her parents but was having a series of meetings with her father with disaster management people. She asked if Iran was one of our case studies. I said no, but it could be. I suggested I send her the questionnaire and she could see if she could somehow use it in her research or get her contacts to apply it for me.

Dzung, the team leader, emailed me to say we were having a briefing meeting in the hotel that evening and were due to meet people in the provincial government at 9 pm tomorrow. I emailed back to say I was in Heathrow. He said you should be here. I emailed back to say I only got the contract late last night and had come as soon as I could. I'd get into Cam Ranh airport at 11am. Come to the hotel and someone will meet you, he said in a more friendly way.

I pass the flight reading World Bank stuff, Mary Beard on Rome and the

Welcome dish

Lonely Planet guide on Vietnam. The premier economy seats are comfortable and spacious and all filled with elderly grey-haired couples my age on the 'holiday of a lifetime'. In Hanoi I took the shuttle bus between international and domestic terminals and caught the Vietnamese Airlines flight to Cam Ranh.

There was a longer wait than I needed in Hanoi but I was relaxed and sat for an hour people watching in the departure lounge before going through to the gate. There were lots of people but a nice Vietnamese lady let me into the queue. The babble of Vietnamese can be strident, but when people are chattering quietly it's rather nice. I found a bar and ordered vegetable noodles for breakfast and got chicken, with a café au lait to wash it down. I got on the Internet while waiting and Ghazala called me and described how their skiing holiday was going and how well the boys were doing. It's a short haul to Cam Ranh and I regret not getting a window seat as we are flying down the coast. I find a taxi and drive the 40 minutes north along the coast. Half finished luxury hotels line the route, built on sand dunes. This is going to be a major resort.

Finally I'm in the hotel – the Intercontinental – on the 17th floor overlooking the beach and the turquoise Bay of Nha Trang. Dzung emails me and tells me we have a meeting with the construction department at 2 pm, so I shower, shave and change.

View from my balcony of the 17th Floor

The meeting goes well, in the sense I don't fall asleep. Huyen, an engineer from the World Bank in Hanoi, has come with me and is translating. She is responsible for the urban planning section so she has questions. We learn that most of the houses that collapsed or were badly damaged were flimsy built temporary structures and most have already been rebuilt. They show us approved plans for two housing types – both small; one of 21 m² and the other of 25 m². They also explain the system of compensation and approval or certification of the works. What I want to know is what proportion of people adopted one of these recommended types and what proportion either built back the same or built back better. They don't seem to know.

We return to the hotel and I get an hour's rest before we meet to debrief in the lobby. I tell Dzung that I'd like to speak to someone in the Red Cross. The people we saw today said the Red Cross are coordinating compensation payments. I listened to the others, Alan, Matteo and Sujit who are reporting on irrigation, agriculture and transport. They seem to know what they're talking about and it's interesting.

After the debrief we get cars to a local restaurant and meet people from the provincial government, but the head man sends his apologies that he has an emergency meeting. The food is fantastic and I enjoy learning about my

Nha Trang beach with traditional 'corracle' type round fishing boat

colleagues. At some point I talk with Alan, Sujit about retirement. They both say they are cutting down on consultancy or would like to. They both also work for the Asian Development Bank and Alan says he'd like to travel less. Sujit says that after he retired 2 or 3 years ago he is doing much less. But what to do after you retire, Alan asks. Sujit says his life is still very full and describes a road trip he made with his daughter from Delhi, where they live, to Calcutta to visit relatives. They stayed three months. He has 50 first cousins. I only have one child myself, I married late, he says, but most of my relatives have big families. So I am a driver now and I've been helping supervise renovations to my daughter's home. He says he is planning more road trips in his 4x4.

Alan says he'd like to buy a place in France to do up. With land and a wood. I think about Leveret Croft and say don't leave it till you retire. Why, he asked. Well it's so much more tiring at 65 than 55, I say. Alan says he has to keep working. I say I don't mean give up consultancy, just start the retirement project now. Alan says he and his wife went to Provence last year looking, so in a sense he started already.

I decide to walk back to the hotel and Alan joins me. The sea front is like Blackpool illuminations and I stop to buy flip-flops in a roadside shop. I get to bed early and ring Scharlie.

Our party gathers outside the District offices in Ninh Hòa

Thursday 15 March

I wake at one and can't get back to sleep till three but luckily go off again. I wake at dawn and open the curtains. There are already people at the beach and I feel inspired to go for a swim. I leave my shorts and T-shirt on one of the hotel loungers and walk into the warm China Sea and out beyond the breakers and swim. Back on the beach and a Vietnamese man greets me and asked me where I'm from and says he lives in California. I'm Vietnamese, he says proudly and shakes my hand. The sand is inviting and I remember running Choroni and set off jogging. I go awhile and turn back. It feels good but suddenly I feel a sharp pain in my right calf and realise I pulled a muscle. Oh dear what time for this to happen. I'm massage in the water but realise it's bad. So I hobble back to my room and lie on the bed with two cold drink cans under my calf muscle.

I get to breakfast and don't feel like eating. I sit with Mateo and tell him about the problem with my leg and ask if he'll try and get the data I need if I don't go interviewing today. I spend the day in my room working on the housing data and my section of the report. If I accept the figures I been given I can report on the damage and recover reconstruction costs easily. Compensation seems only to have been paid to people whose homes were destroyed. Only

Hyundai-Vinashin shipyard, My Giang, Ninh Phuoc, Ninh Hòa

2% of affected houses were completely destroyed by the typhoon whereas over half or 63,000 suffered substantial or heavy damage. We were told by people in the Department of construction that nearly everyone had rebuilt their homes only four months after the storm and only a few were waiting for a more propitious moment. I wondered if they were just referring to the 2% who got compensated.

Vietnam seems to be booming. I read growth rate is 7-8% per year and there seem to be lots of jobs. But average income for most is low and consumer goods, especially cars, are expensive.

I work 12 hours and send my draft off to Keiko for comment. She replies almost immediately that the losses I calculated for house contents are considered as damages and not losses by the Bank and, more importantly, that the report needs to be read as if it comes from the government. So I need to change the tone from my usual outsider critic. No problem. I order room service – tomato soup and stir-fried chicken and rice with a beer from the fridge.

Wrecked prawn hatchery in Cho Ninh Phuoc

Friday 16 March

We meet a 8am in the lobby and are assigned to cars. I'm with Matteo and Huyen and we are going to sites where we can see agricultural damage and housing recovery. We drive north along the coast, past the famous Cham Towers, to the town of Ninh Hoa. There was more damage in the North and as we drive I can see signs of damage to flimsy tin roofs and some tiles missing, but there is much less visible damage than I expected. We go first to the office of the municipal government and meet people from the economic division who are going to come with us. We divide groups here and Alan and Sujit head off to investigate irrigation and roads.

Our party goes up the coast away to a peninsula with the huge Hyundai-Vinashin shipyard. This area has recently been rezoned from agriculture to industry. There are demolished houses that don't look as though they've been damaged in the storm and Huyen confirms that they have been condemned and the families relocated. There are one or two still occupied and I wonder why. Perhaps the men are still working clearing the land or building access roads for the Japanese power plant that is coming here.

We reach the village of Cho Ninh Phuoc and out of courtesy call in at the new commune office building, which has also been relocated from the

Embankment made from coral from Aceh, Indonesia

industrial zone. There is clearly tight government control right down to the local level and this calling in to announce our visit is a pattern we follow all day.

We return to the village and drive along the coast to a series of shrimp hatcheries that we are told were badly damaged in the storm. We can see that the superstructure has gone and the plastic pipework smashed and all that remains are shallow concrete pools, now dry. This family went bankrupt, we are told. People take loans and are not able to keep up the payments after the storm. The family next door has managed to survive and has rebuilt a temporary superstructure and we can hear the pumps working.

Driving back through the village it's obvious the houses on more exposed sites suffered more damage. A number of houses are being repaired. They are generally simple single or two-storey buildings; some have concrete frames, most are just block work. Those with single block work walls and tin roofs seem to have been the ones that failed in the storm. There is no time to stop and I rather unsuccessfully try and photograph out of the car window.

We drive to promontory to look at new shrimp under construction. I notice that the enclosing embankment is coral and point this out to Huyen. She says the owner imported the material from Aceh in Indonesia from the clear up after the 2004 Indian Ocean tsunami. I can hardly believe it. But there were

Matteo and Chau discuss agricultural recovery and what they'll do to clear the forests

House recently rebuilt by the District Government

Traditional Cham long house

large ships capable of carrying bulk materials like debris in the shipyard and when I look at a map later, it's not so far.

Lunch is in Ninh Hoa. Our party seems to divide naturally, with the English speakers down one end of the table. I like the food and follow Chau's example. She says in the North, in Hanoi, they have rice last. The fish is delicious, as is the pickled cucumber. There is very tender slow-cooked pork, which I don't try. And to finish we have pineapple and tea.

From here we drive west into the hills and pick up a young woman who will be our guide in Khánh Vĩnh District. From here is not that far to Cambodia. We stop in a forest and get out of the cars to see the damage to the acacia trees that a used in paper-making. We are told that about half the trees were damaged and we can see fallen trees both sides of the road, one in the government-owned forest, the other owned by a man in the USA. Someone asks why the fallen trees haven't been cleared. They are all about 6 inches in diameter and not ready for harvesting, we're told. But the main reason is that there is only one paper factory in the province and there is a glut in timber and it is uneconomic to clear the fallen trees. In other places they are gradually clearing up and clearly it's a big job that will take time because of the difficulty of access through the fallen.

Alan discusses the business of growing pomelo and the impact of the storm

It clouds over feels threatening. I'm taken to see a new house that has been rebuilt by the government and introduced to the lady owner. She seems to be a female head of house, although I'm not sure. The house is single-storey and about 4x4 metres and built in the traditional local style with a simple porch. We are told that her previous home was totally destroyed and we are shown the pile of debris. The house has an uninsulated tin roof and a simple metal door and window shutter. It cost 40 million VND, the government built it and she was given the keys, we are told. The house next door is similar but this neighbour lost her roof, which the government replaced. Her house has a crude timber door and wooden shutter over the window.

I'm intrigued by the long house next door. I'm told it's a traditional design amongst the ethnic group of the area, the Cham Raglai people, but there is no compensation for this type of communal house. The timbers are huge dark hardwood and look ancient. Someone is repairing the roof with new tiles and has nearly finished. I imagine the walls of flimsy screens. The floor of the house is built metre above ground level and we are told people traditionally would pull up their ladder at night. There used to be wild animals in the forest and snakes. Later I muse on the dramatic changes Vietnam and the whole of South-East Asia is engulfed in and how wildlife doesn't stand a chance. Maybe

The farmer show Sujit and me round his house

these beautiful longhouses and the culture they represent are more enduring or maybe this renovation is exceptional.

I also wonder how representative the house we have just been shown is of the 2000 homes that are supposed to have been rebuilt throughout the province. This area has a higher proportion of collapsed houses than other districts so it must have been badly hit the people here in the highlands must be poorer than on the coast. We drive on to visit a couple whose orchard of pomelo trees was badly hit. The man tells as he had 600 trees on 2 hectares of land. Only 100 were left undamaged, 150 were knocked over but he saved them and was fertilising them to make strong again, and 350 had been lost. He also lost 48 of his 50 Durian trees.

He invited us in and Alan and Matteo asked him about his business. He said the trees were six years old and had begun bearing after four years. He was paying back the loans he taken to install the irrigation system and build a house when the storm hit. He'd bought new plans to replace the ones lost and they were lined up outside waiting to go in. We had learnt that the rate of interest on the loan was 0.9% per month, which seemed high and we wanted to know if there was any debt relief for farmers like him that been affected by the storm. He said there was no government help. Dzung interrupted to say we shouldn't

Rearing ducks is a big part of the local economy

be asking this kind of question; that this was a touchy subject and we should be sensitive to his feelings. The man seemed most ready to talk and was clearly a very emotionally strong character. Maybe Dzung was more worried about the feeling of the government official who was accompanying us. Nevertheless, we stop our line of questioning, just when it was getting interesting.

I was interested in his house and asked if the round was new. He invited me upstairs. It had rough wooden board floor and steel shutters that open to the breeze and a view over his trees. There was a mattress with a mosquito net and a clothes rack and nothing else. He said he had 10 to 12 people working for him and he could crop all year as the fruit reach maturity. Seeing what he had in his home – an old TV and fridge and a motor scooter outside – I think maybe I need to rethink the possessions people might have had in their homes when the storm hit and how much in value they had lost since I had been dramatically over estimating.

We drove back and went to my room and after a hot bath I was wiped out. I didn't bother eating, as we'd have a big lunch.

Room service in the hotel as I'm unable to walk far

Saturday 17 March

We met in the lobby at 9 to debrief. Dzung is a little ineffective and gets confused He produces sheets of new figures and says there are important for us all but it's not clear how he'll get them to us. Alan asked about the translation and Dzung says that there is too much to translate. Alan goes off to make copies and we sit with Chau who translates the headings and the main points in the text.

Dzung says we have got to get our slides for his presentation to the provincial government meeting on Wednesday morning back to him by Monday. People protest and we settle on Tuesday at 5 pm. Dzung then says that I will be coordinating the report. I feel I have to say something. So I pipe up that I will help with the report, but I'm not prepared to take the lead so people should send their work to him since he is the team leader He says Keiko had led him to believe I would be putting the report together. I said she wasn't paying me enough to take responsibility for the report. I regretted saying it immediately. I'll probably have to do it anyway. Later in my room I discover I haven't got the breakdown of housing damaged by district. I was sure we had been given it at our first meeting and Huyen had hung onto it for some reason. I couldn't ask because she'd shot off after lunch yesterday and was away for the weekend.

Hugh Van Es's iconic image of the helicopter escape from a Saigon rooftop on April 29 1975

So I had to email Dzung and say I was missing housing data broken down by district and might have to go back to the Department of Construction. Dzung was shirty with me; not surprising since I pissed him off about refusing to take on the report.

I worked all day till 8 pm when I rang Alan to see if he wanted to go for a meal. He said he been already, so I walked down to the sea. My leg was still painful and stiff, so I went back to my room and had room service again and do some more work till after 11. One of my difficulties is that I don't quite understand the purpose of the World Bank report we are writing. In housing, report that I'm writing, I can report on the total level of damage and what the government is doing in terms of targeting compensation to those most in need i.e. those whose homes were badly damaged or destroyed and who are poor or in special need. This is hugely short of what would be needed to rebuild and repair all houses and replace the contents that were lost, so obviously people are expected to meet the difference themselves. They seem to be coping extremely well. Vietnamese are very industrious and entrepreneurial. They've cleared up quickly after the typhoon and got people rehoused. Given the reality of their limited resources, they are doing well. The only thing they might have done, since the banks of government-owned, is to

North Vietnamese tank breaks through into the American Embassy

target resources at supporting small businesses, for example by deferring loan repayments or providing more generous credit facilities. But we may not have got the whole story about livelihood support since Dzung closed down this line of questioning yesterday.

Sunday 18 March
As predicted by my Norwegian weather site the day dawned bright and sunny and despite a rather sleepless night I was down to breakfast soon after seven and chatted briefly to Alan. I stoke up at breakfast and have a bowl of Vietnamese rice or noodles, followed by an English breakfast, then mango and walnut and dried fruit, washed down with tomato juice and orange juice and tea and coffee. What a glutton.

I worked the rest of the morning and rang Alan and arranged to meet for lunch. We walked down the promenade to the nearest restaurant and shared avocado and shrimp. I had a beer and on the way back stopped at the hotel lounges on the beach and did 30 minutes tanning. I fell asleep in my room and woke feeling groggy and watched a documentary called "The last days in Vietnam" about the American evacuation from Saigon in 1975. It was very

Rickshaw biccycles

emotional and the men interviewed – the CIA section heads, the Marines, Navy captains and Vietnamese now living in America, were all still upset by the shock of what they saw as the betrayal of South Vietnam. Perhaps as many as 200 to 300,000 Vietnamese, some of whom had been working for the Americans or had been in the South Vietnamese army or government, managed to get out. Those that stayed were sent to re-education camps. One had done 10 years hard labour. I read later that it was the South that had invented "re-education".

In the long term the country has benefited from reunification. The film made clear that the USA had assumed there would be an enduring partition into North and South. In 1973 the Paris Accord had ended hostilities and was only signed by the South Vietnamese government because Nixon had promised to come to their aid with full force if North Vietnam didn't honour the agreement. In the film Kissinger made it clear that North Vietnam regarded Nixon as a mad man who would unleash a renewed bombing campaign and they were terrified of him. Then Watergate happened, Nixon was gone and Gerald Ford was seen as a reasonable man, so the North Vietnamese immediately invaded

School run home Vietnamese style

and swept south. Graham Martin, the US Ambassador in South Vietnam, was a Cold War warrior who had lost his only son in the war and wasn't going to give in to defeatist talk. South Vietnam had a huge army supported by American resources, so Martin refused to hear talk of evacuation by ship and left things too late. A group of CIA and marine officers Black Ops airlift was begun by American military, without Martin's knowledge, flying people out on returning cargo planes. When North Vietnam shelled the airport. Suddenly there were no options left other helicopters. Congress refused Gerald Ford's request to $800 million.

In April 1975 there were harrowing scenes of people fleeing. But Ambassador Martin procrastinated in the final 24 hours, refusing to agree to the tamarind tree in the car park being cut down to allow the big Chinook helicopters to land, saying that the tree was a symbol of America's steadfastness to defend the south. And yet, with over 40 years hindsight, the country is better for unification and the extreme threat of communism didn't materialise.

That evening Alan and I sallied fourth again and rented a rickshaw to take us to a photographic gallery I wanted to visit. Alan was outraged when the man charged us 400,000 VND, about £13. We settled on 100,000 after an argument. But we couldn't find the gallery we'd come to see, despite using Alan's iPad and Google maps, so we gave up and went to dinner. We chatted. Alan was born in Malawi in the 50s. His father was District Commissioner in the Northern Province. He had gone to boarding school in England when he was 11. His closest friend was one of their servants' sons who had died of AIDS. Over lunch we talked about the company he worked for and I described CAR's structure. He immediately said it was inherently unfair. In his company there was a very flat structure with 28 owners who were paid a salary plus bonuses and the founder of the company in North-West Canada had enshrined the idea of paying a 30% annual bonus to all employees.

Monday 19 March
I was first down to breakfast, soon after six. I have a meeting this morning at nine with people in the Red Cross responsible for administering three UNDP housing schemes. Their priority, they said, was emergency response followed by livelihood support and then housing. Donations and aid was coordinated centrally but priorities were set by the local authorities, the Peoples'

Commune Committee in each hamlet, who determined how badly each house was damaged and whether the household met the eligibility criteria or poor, near-poor or disadvantaged. A contract for a group of houses was let to one of two designs approved by the Ministry of Construction to a budget of $22,000 for each house. Typically 50% was paid when the foundations were completed and 50% on completion. The money was paid into the National Bank and the builder had to go to a bank branch with a certificate to get paid. Technical help was provided to local builders by DWF a French NGO. The same eligibility criteria of damage and financial circumstance was applied to repairs and houses that were 50 to 70% severely damage got $250 and those with heavy damage 30 to 50% got $160. I asked if this was enough to do the repairs. They said no, it was a contribution to the cost. So is there a big backlog of repairs because most people can't afford it, I asked. No they said most of the repairs have been done. I asked if the same opportunity had been taken to build that better with rebuild and they said no, not really. Payments were quite flexible though and people could claim compensation even if the work had already been done.

The man in charge had left most of the talking to a lady who had been in charge of housing. The deputy chair, another intelligent lady, answered my

Long Than Gallery

questions about how the majority, who didn't receive help, had faired. She said they had borrowed from relatives or the bank or on the black market to finish their homes in time for the Vietnamese New Year. It is the most important date in the Vietnamese calendar and celebrates the arrival of spring, she said. Vietnamese prepare by cooking special food and cleaning and getting the house ready. It is a time for greeting guests and forgetting about troubles past and looking forward to a better year. So it was important for people and the authorities to rebuild repair homes in time. I also asked her about house contents. She said it was difficult to verify who had owned what before the event and how much it was worth. So no compensation was paid for lost or damaged possessions.

I asked if they had learnt anything and if they would do things differently. She said, yes that the standard designs offered by the Ministry of Construction should have taken comfort and amenity into account and that better house

Salt gathering (Long Than Photo)

plans would need funding from other additional sources that needed mobilising, only in this way would they improve housing in Vietnam, she said. I thought better building control systems, with stricter building codes and home insurance, might also be effective in the longer term.

While we've been talking the boss had been making notes and he launched into a speech, the gist of which was that many more homes could be damaged by future storms and that the government should begin a programme of improving all existing homes. He also thought that after a disaster the government should prioritise livelihoods but they have done little after Typhoon Damrey. I would have liked to talk more with him but Nhat, my interpreter, wouldn't translate what he'd said and seemed much keener on making his own points than in translating my questions. So I gave up and thanked them warmly.

Back in the car I suggested they dropped me at the Long Than Gallery. Long Than is a Vietnamese photographer in black-and-white recommended in my guide. They found it fairly easily and told me to get a taxi back. It was a classy

Woman collecting water (Long Than Gallery)

gallery. There were two ancient Lambretta scooters in perfect condition on display either end of a long low with heavy teak table. They were in immaculate condition – one cream and one pale green. A lady welcomed me who spoke a little English and let me wander around looking at the photographs – quite large prints of Vietnamese scenes. There were some of young Vietnamese girls in traditional white dress and one of a beautiful girl lying half naked in a hammock. But the ones I liked most were of the salt pans in the Hon Khoi Salt Field showing conical piles of white salt being gathered by women in conical leaf hats. There was also one of a woman collecting water. The river had seemingly fractured into a myriad of sparkling jewels and the bank was basaltic lava that had solidified into blocks like black Pontefract cakes.

I asked how much they cost, thinking to buy one. She handed me a price list. They range from $150-$350 depending on the size. I thought a moment and said, I am afraid that's too much for me. I regretted it immediately, but I also couldn't decide which one I like best. I asked her if she was the photographer's wife and she said yes. The lady called a taxi for me and one eventually came and took me back to the hotel. He charged less than one 10th of what the pedalo drivers had charged us last night for a much longer journey.

I spent the afternoon working until nearly five when Alan rang and asked if I'd like to go for a swim before the sun went. So I pulled on my trunks and sallied forth. Getting across the dual carriageway is exciting but we had the services of lollipop boy from the hotel, who strode into the traffic with us trying to keep in step. The water was warm and milky and although I had to be careful not to strain my calf muscle further, I enjoyed it. It soon got dark and we headed back and later that evening went down the promenade to the first restaurant and had a quick meal.

Alan is based in Bangladesh working on hydrology projects – irrigation and his company, Northwest Hydraulic Consultants (NHC), is doing a lot of work on river defences. Bangladesh is a most interesting place, not a tourist destination necessarily, he says. It's very entrepreneurial and has a growth rate similar to that of Vietnam. The country encourages foreign investment by making it easy for foreign companies to establish in Bangladesh without needing local ownership and it's also easy to take money out. Then on the downside there is endemic corruption. My son is working there for a huge NGO called BRAC, the largest NGO in the world, established in Bangladesh in 1972 at independence. It employs over 100,000 people and began as a rural development charity and moved into health and then micro-finance. Alan said it might go down the line of becoming an ethical company and various parts were already operating in this way. His son had started there as an intern and now was on a sixth month contract. Alan hoped he would go back to Sussex and finish his degree in international development. We talked about South America. I told him about living in Venezuela in the 70s and how I'd gone exploring and it was only now I realised how special it was. I also said one of my only regrets was not accepting Ian Edwards's invitation to go to East Africa in 1980.

Tuesday 20 March
I had an early breakfast and worked all morning responding to a request from Dzung to edit my slides and provide summary tables. By 1pm I had finished and was ready to do my final interviews with the Department of Planning and Investment. We set off in the cars again and drive north a mile or so to more government offices. All these offices, at provincial, district and commune level, are cut from the same mould - all with a big red banner and gold lettering. We wait a while – it seems that the man we come to see has gone to Hanoi

Ahmad tries to ask questions about economic planning

for a meeting. Finally we are ushered up four flights to a meeting room with a bust of Ho Chi Minh, the father of the nation. An elderly man explains he has been asked, at the last minute, to meet us but has no information. A second younger man joins him. Huyen explains the purpose of our visit and Ahmad, the Economist from the World Bank, gently asks questions about investment planning. The young man begins a tirade. I gather he's not answering the question when Viet, the local World Bank economist, intervenes. It begins a shouting match. It's fascinating listening to the raised voices. In Europe this would be a full-blown row, here it's normal meeting discourse. The sound level rises as Chau and Huyen at either end of the table try to interpret for us. In the end Sujit and I learn little. However, I discover, almost inadvertently, that the urban development plan also covers housing, but that social housing is provided through a levy on private developments, rather like affordable housing in the UK, and the plan is a set of rules rather than an investment plan with a budget.

I get back to the hotel with a new idea about calculating reconstruction costs in housing. I've been applying a simple single price of 57 million VND to all houses needing rebuild or repair and adjusting for the level of damage. But I realise most houses are much bigger than this and will therefore cost

Provincial Government offices

more to fix. I remember I was told the range of sizes of existing houses at our first meeting and I can calculate a basic price per square metre. This means that I can set different costs for different house types in each district and calculate a more detail reconstruction cost table. The problem is that this new figure comes out twice what was calculated by the Provincial Department of Flood Control. Their figures give the number of homes damaged as 118,000. I have finally got figures for population in each district for 2016 and from the Internet find average household size has been falling in Vietnam from 5.8 in 1998 to about 3.5 today. This gives me a total estimate of 346,791 houses in the Province. If both figures are correct this would mean that one in three houses were damaged. I can't believe this is true and am perplexed about the discrepancy, but there is nothing I can do. The others have accepted the damage data provided by the Province and maybe I should just do the same. But then what am I here for? It's a dilemma. I get to bed early after a quick meal with Alan in the hotel. We talk about Brexit. His wife voted to leave and he voted to stay, but he's rather excited at the prospect of how we might manage outside the EU and the opportunities it creates.

The Deputy Governor of the Province Dao Long Thén

Wednesday 21 March

Today we present our report and findings to the Provincial, District and Departmental reps. The offices are imposing and well built and we trog upstairs again. A large number of delegates are gathered in the conference room. The vice-chair of the provincial government, a chubby affable man with a big smile and direct manner greets us and Alan especially since they met in Australia. He controls the meeting well. It seems more than anything else an exercise in consensus building. Dzung presents our findings, then the chairman of each of the badly affected districts gets to speak, then the heads of each of the relevant departments. I learn a lot from what the head of the Department of Agriculture and Rural Development has to say. He says that the most affected sector was fisheries accounting for 10 trillion VND losses in output from badly damaged lobster and prawns hatcheries and fish ponds. This is a big part of the local economy. Orchards were also badly hit and forestry although this is much less important. It will affect the province's GDP for 2018 but is offset by an increase in construction, he says. More than anything investors need greater security to invest in new technology – for example relocating fish farms to deeper water offshore and investing impact

Last day on on hotel loungers on Nha Trang beach

irrigation for highly valuable crops rather than canals for rice cultivation. I'm thinking insurance when the vice-chairman says that some bigger fish farms had insurance but since the wind speed reached a maximum of only 115 km per hour rather than 120, the French insurers didn't pay. I think they need a better government-sponsored insurance system for businesses and possibly homes, which would drive investment and raise standards.

We get back to the hotel and debrief in the lobby. Someone asked me to hang back after we finish. I'd already been primed by Keiko that Dzung has decided to write the report himself and that the Bank wants to renegotiate my contract. He said he was thinking 13 days. I said I understood and would let him know. I get back to my room and write an email saying I added my hours and it came to 15 days. I packed and checked out by 12.30. I worked in the lobby for half an hour then checked my bag and came down to the beach to sunbathe till 4.30 when we are due to leave for the airport.

We take two taxis to the airport and Alan and I go for a meal. He goes to Burger King and I choose Vietnamese Home Cooking where I order a bowl of rice and vegetables. He joins me, there was nowhere to sit at the Burger King. I board before him because he wanted to send an email, then he came and sat next to me. I read for a short while and then fell asleep. I am dead tired.

Taxi to the airport

We part company at the luggage carousel and vow to keep in touch. I liked him and much enjoyed our many conversations.

I waited a while for the shuttle bus. The departure terminal was heaving with people but I found the business class check-in and then the business class lounge and settled down with an orange juice and watermelon for two hours, watching Michael Caine in the Quiet American set in Vietnam in the 50s. Then it was time to board and I was pampered with hot and cold running stewardesses bearing wine.

I would so much have liked to have seen more of this country. The trip was also last-minute and Scharlie would have been upset if I'd stayed an extra week. I don't suppose I'd get the chance to come again. I like Vietnam – it was clean as Sujit pointed out, comparing Vietnam favourably with home in India, and is well built, as Alan said. But for me it's the impression people give of confidence – they're good at their jobs and know where they're going.

I watched three classic Vietnamese films on the way home. The first "Floating Lives" begins with a woman being assaulted and chased by a group of women shouting that will serve her right for stealing their husbands. She escapes and lives with a man and his children on a boat in the marshes of the Mekong Delta herding ducks in rice paddies. It's a sad poignant tale of love withheld

Still from movie "Floating Lives"

that is a final happy ending with father and daughter reconciled and living happily in the village.

The second is set in the 60s with all the young man in flared trousers. It's called "Hanoi in the Season of Bird Nesting". Again it's a love story between a young engaged couple caught between traditional family approval and the directives of the state about where young people should live and work. The boy's father is a high-ranking academic who fought at Dien Bien Phu and who hates corruption and patronage, and the girls mother runs a black market shop and does deals and expects favours. Their young love fades and the boy falls in love and marries the girl's best friend. What comes across is the tension created by the imposition of communist planning and the effervescent commercial zeal of the Vietnamese. You can see how this is playing out today in Vietnam with the contradictions created by state control and dynamic market forces. The other thing that comes across strongly is the equal status of young men and women and the traditional values of the older generation when women deferred to men.

Again you can see this in modern-day Vietnam where women and men are formally awarded equal status based on their talent and ability rather than gender, but where women tend to play a subordinate role in the hierarchy. Nevertheless it is refreshingly egalitarian and as gender equal as Britain.

The final film is called "Moon at the Bottom of the Well" about a successful teacher who devotes herself to her health-conscious husband and is frustrated by his lack of passion. We landed before I managed to finish it. In all the films, including "The Quiet American", the women are sensitive, beautiful, elegant and devoted and the men screw things up by their arrogance, ideals, ambition and lack of charity. There are stark differences in lifestyle between the four films in terms of how well off the families are and what possessions they have. Yet the women in all the films somehow create elegance and tranquillity in their homes with plants, flowers, neatness, tidiness and caring hands that the men seem to undermine with their boorish ways. The countryside is so different from Europe and the UK. It's farmed and used obviously but it isn't manicured. It's clean, in the sense that there is no litter or destruction, but the uncultivated parts are untamed. The Vietnamese are generally slim and fit looking and the women are so elegant in their simple trousers and blouse or longer traditional dress; elegant in the every day tasks are washing, folding bedding, dressing and serving food.

I have seen so little of life in Vietnam on this visit and have a thirst to know more. I can see how young Frenchman and young Americans in their turn fell in love with Vietnam and beautiful young Vietnamese women. Graham Greene gives a line to, is Fowler, the journalist, in The Quiet American, played by Michael Caine – You get to know a lot about Vietnam in the first few days, the rest you have to learn by living it.

Traditional Vietnamese dress

Rice is still the staple crop

Rowing with her feet

www.ingramcontent.com/pod-product-compliance
Lightning Source LLC
Chambersburg PA
CBHW042007100426
42738CB00037B/30